SCHIRMER'S LIBRARY
OF MUSICAL CLASSICS

Vol. 2060

Dmitri Kabalevsky

Easy Variations
on Folk Themes, Op. 51

For Piano

ISBN 978-1-4234-0849-9

G. SCHIRMER, Inc.

DISTRIBUTED BY

HAL•LEONARD®
CORPORATION
7777 W. BLUEMOUND RD. P.O. BOX 13819 MILWAUKEE, WI 53213

DMITRI KABALEVSKY (1904-1987)

Dmitri Kabalevsky was born in St. Petersburg, Russia on December 30, 1904. He received a liberal education from his father. The young Dmitri excelled in the arts, painting and writing poetry, in addition to being an aspiring pianist. However, not unlike other parents of artists at the time, Kabalevsky's father wished him to pursue a career outside of the arts. In 1922, Kabalevsky took the entrance exam to the Engels Socio-Economic Science Institute, where he would likely pursue a career in mathematics or economics, like his father. Young Dmitri never enrolled in the school, however, and was determined to pursue a career in music. He studied and taught piano at the Scriabin Institute, where he composed works for his students, establishing a lifelong interest in providing young musicians with quality literature. In 1925, Kabalevsky went to the Moscow Conservatory to continue studies in piano and composition. While there, he composed the first works to be recognized internationally: the Piano Concerto No. 1 (1928), and the Sonatina in C major (1930) for piano. He eventually became a full professor at the Moscow Conservatory in 1939.

Kabalevsky had a successful career as a composer in the USSR due to a conservative aesthetic temperament, largely avoiding the difficulties encountered by his contemporaries Sergei Prokofiev and Dmitri Shostakovich, while still producing a large body of fresh and original music. Even so, following the 1948 party decree on music in the Soviet Union, Kabalevsky's works became significantly more lyrical in quality. His large body of works for student pianists were vital elements of Soviet music education, and became welcome additions to teaching literature throughout the world. His later pieces include many large works for chorus and orchestra, for which he remains most known in his native country. Kabalevsky died in Moscow on February 18, 1987.

Contents

EASY VARIATIONS ON FOLK THEMES

1. Five Variations on a Russian Folk Song

Dmitri Kabalevsky

Op. 51, No. 1
(1952)

Theme
Allegro

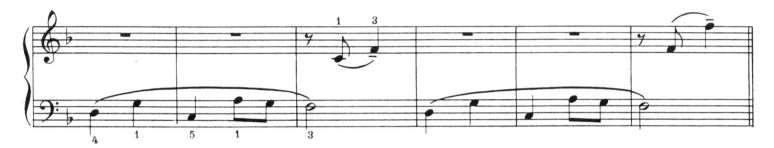

Var. 1

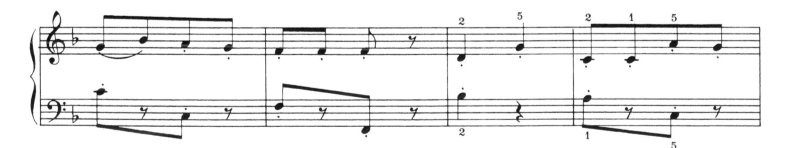

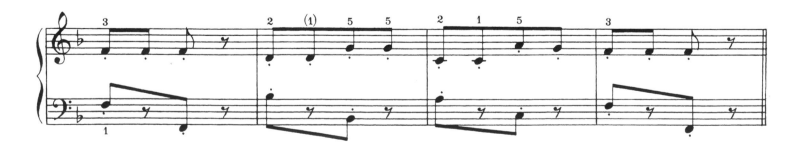

Var. 2

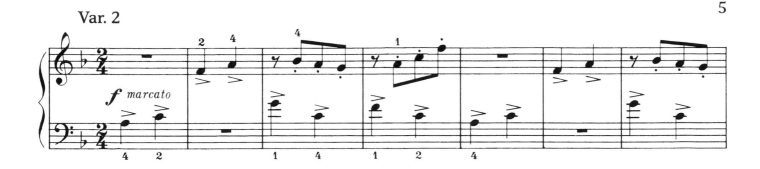

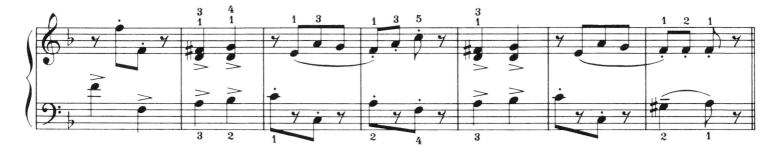

Var. 3

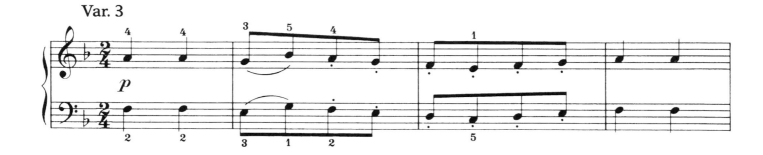

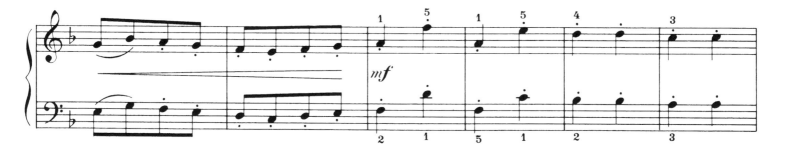

6

Var. 4

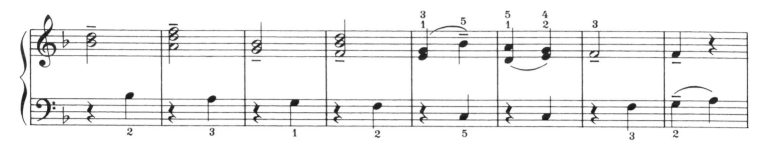

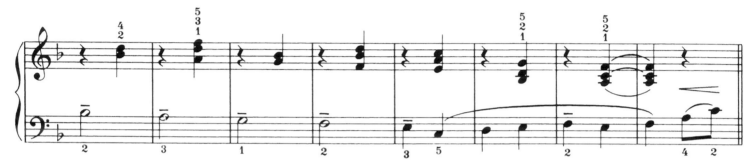

Var. 5

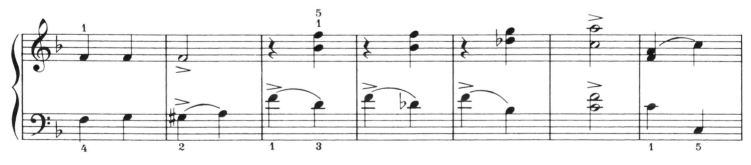

2. Dance Variations on a Russian Folk Song

Op. 51, No. 2
(1952)

Var. 3

Var. 4

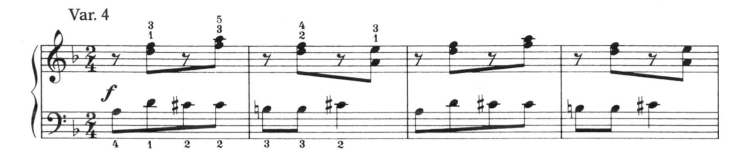

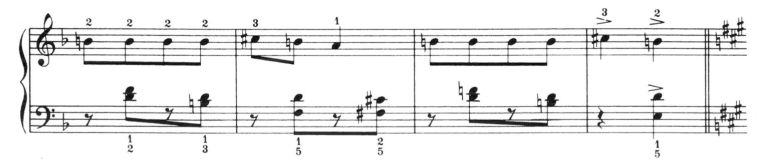

Var. 5

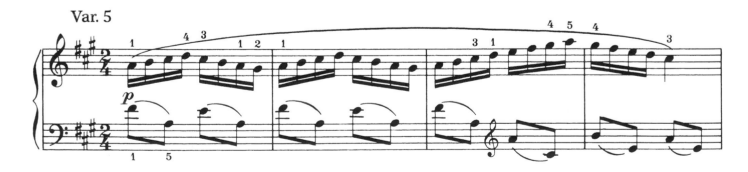

Var. 6

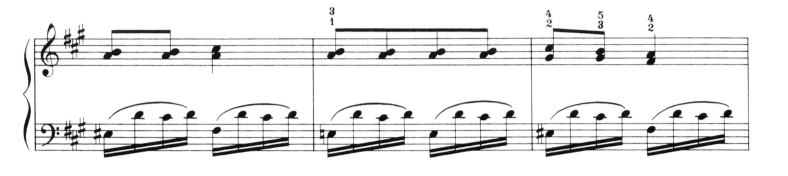

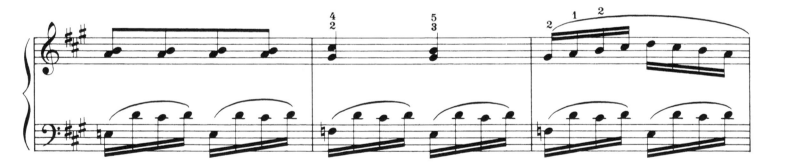

3. "Gray Day" Variations on a Slovakian Folk Song

Theme

Op. 51, No. 3
(1952)

Moderato (♩ = ca. 85)

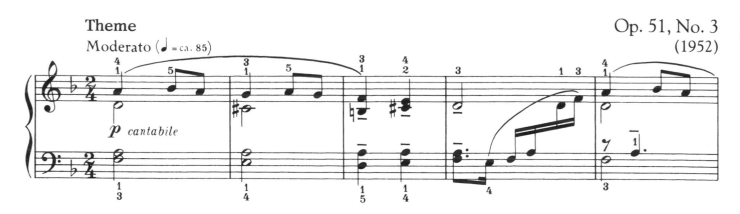

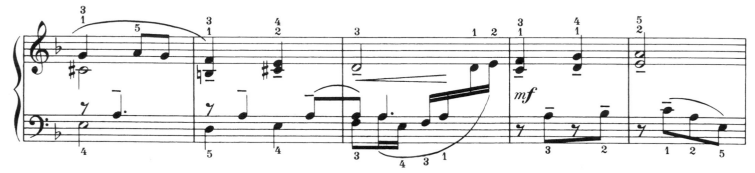

Var. 1

Allegretto giocoso (♩ = ca. 80)

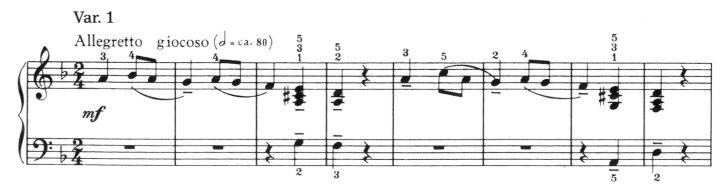

Var. 2

Var. 3

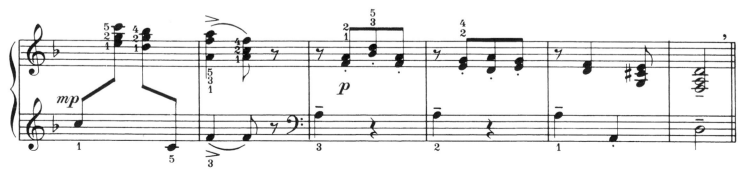

Var. 4

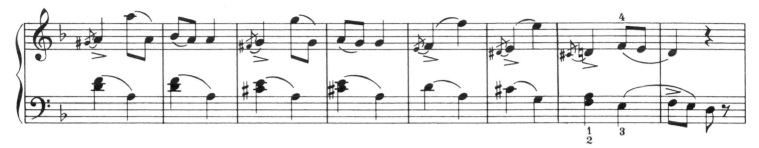

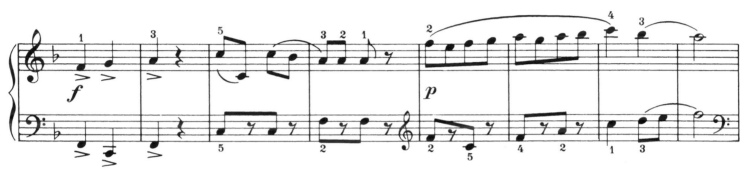

Var. 5

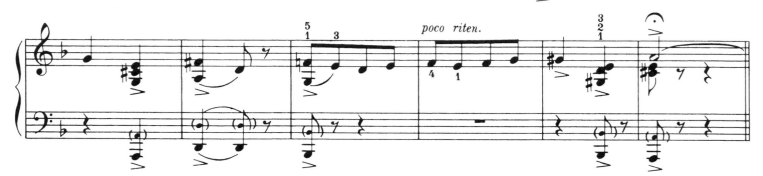

Var. 6 (Coda)

Moderato

4. Seven Cheerful Variations on a Slovakian Folk Song

Op. 51, No. 4
(1952)

Theme
Allegretto scherzando

Var. 1

Var. 2

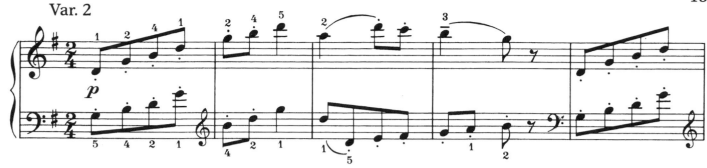

Var. 3

Var. 4

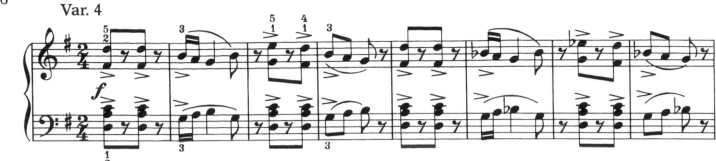

Var. 5

Var. 6

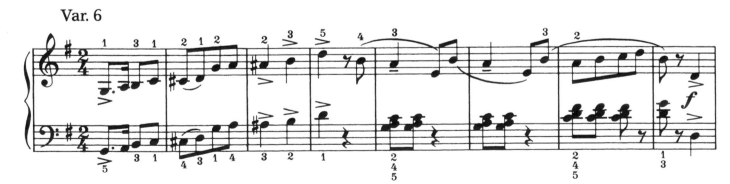

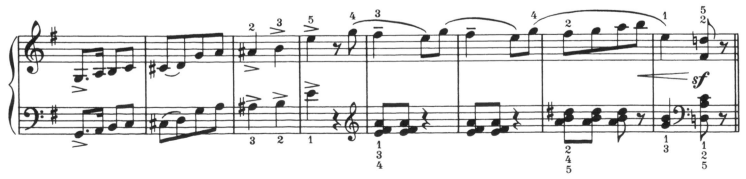

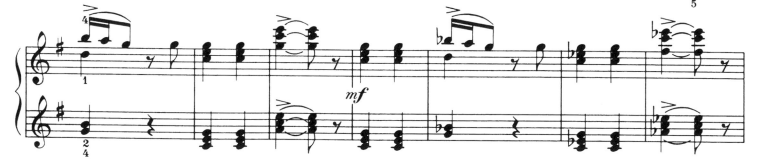

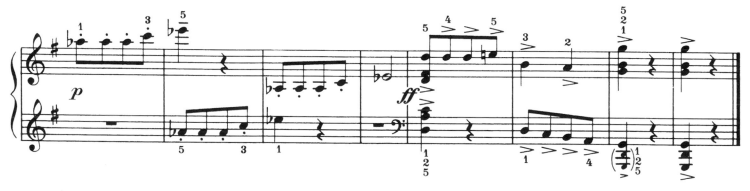

5. Six Variations on a Ukrainian Folk Song

Op. 51, No. 5
(1952)

Theme
Andantino

Var. 1
Poco più mosso

Var. 2

Var. 3

poco   a   poco   cresc.

Var. 4

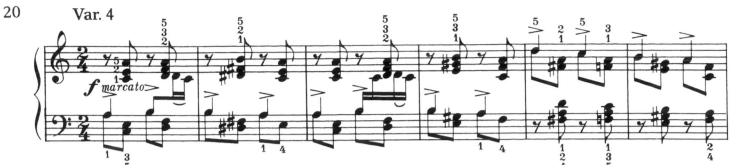

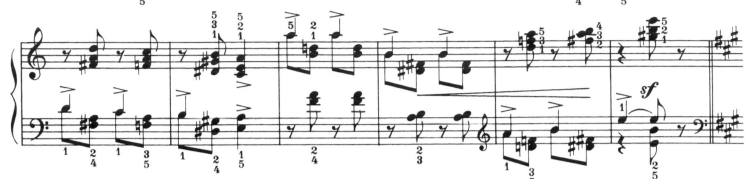

Var. 5

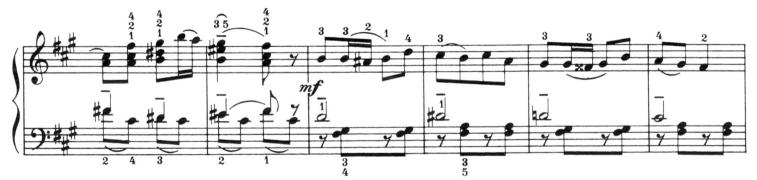

Var. 6

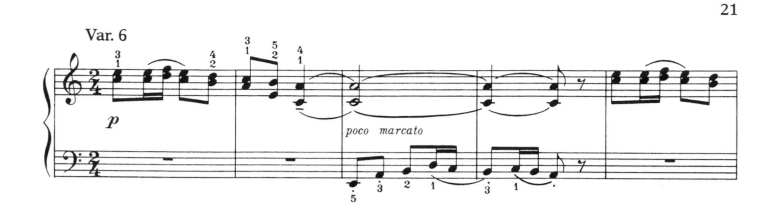